Seen and Heard

Embassy of the Bolivarian Republic of Venezuela
Venezuelan Institute for Culture and Cooperation
in St. Vincent and the Grenadines

International Women's Day, 8 March 2011

Contributors

Alisa Alvis
Narissa Ballantyne
Shanelle Bascombe
Jamillah Burgin
Shonette Bynoe
Peggy Carr
Amanda Frederick
Felicia Gabrielle George
Nelcia Robinson Hazell
Clare Ibberson-John
Janeele Jackson
Janique-Ka John
Nerissa King
Jecinta Hope Knights
Jeneille Lewis
Joyce Peters McKenzie
Natana McLean
Nora Peacock
Debra Providence
Vonnie Roudette
Caroline "booops" Sardine
Olivia Stephens

Seen and Heard

An Anthology
of Art and Poetry
by Vincentian women

SPUYTEN DUYVIL
an imprint of
HOBO JUNGLE PRESS
Woodbury, Connecticut

Published by Spuyten Duyvil Books, an imprint of Hobo Jungle Press
Woodbury, Connecticut 06798
www.hobojungle.org

ISBN 978-0-9829945-2-8

Library of Congress Control Number: 2011923666

Cover: *Strength, Humility of a Black Woman*, Shanelle Bascombe

CONTENTS

FOREWORD

On June 19th, 2009, I had the pleasure of hosting a cultural event entitled, "An Exhibition of Art and Poetry" in the Simon Bolivar Conference Room of the Institute for Culture and Cooperation (IVCC) at the Venezuelan Embassy in St. Vincent and the Grenadines. The unassuming title of the event did not prepare me, or the guests who attended this event, for a most unforgettable evening during which the aesthetics of art and poetry came together to celebrate and consecrate the savoir faire and cultural syncretism of an extraordinary group of Vincentian women.

For me, the poetry that was read and the paintings displayed on that occasion represent the most transcendental expressions of the human condition: the sense of creation that emerges from life experience, the beauty and sensitivity of the women who live amidst the magic waters of the Caribbean, and the common chain that links artists and all of humanity to the wonderful sense of life. For those of us who were fortunate enough to have heard these poems and to have viewed the paintings that accompanied them, they give witness to the beautiful women who live here and grace us with their experiences, dreams and utopias.

Following the event, it was with immense pleasure that the IVCC invited the collaborators, Nelcia Robinson Hazell and Vonnie Roudette, to create a chapbook in support of the poets of St. Vincent and the Grenadines. The objective of this book is to expose the tenacious work of the Vincentian artists who participated in the event to the general public and to confirm their fundamental contribution to a culture of friendship, solidarity and peace throughout the eastern and southern Caribbean region and with all the people of our beautiful blue planet.

Yoel Pérez Marcano
H.E. Ambassador of the Bolivarian Republic of Venezuela
in St. Vincent and the Grenadines

INTRODUCTION

As ideas are conceived, germinate and grow, the birthing of this anthology took just nine months, quietly forming during the first three without our knowing.

In March 2009, the Embassy of the Bolivarian Republic of Venezuela to St. Vincent and the Grenadines, held a series of events to celebrate Women's History Month. On the 20th an event entitled '100 years of Women's Day' was staged there, and I was invited by Empress Modupe Olufunmi-Jacobs to make a presentation on 'Women and Art' among a panel of women. After our presentations, Sister Nelcia Robinson-Hazell approached me saying she had an idea to put together a women's poetry evening. I suggested that to combine visual images with the spoken word may help to present different aspects of women's creativity and acknowledge our ideas as forming meaningful relationships within our daily culture. The idea grew into reality and the event called *Seen and Heard* took place on the 19th of June, hosted by Ambassador Yoel Pérez Marcano at the same Embassy.

That evening, surrounded by 39 expressive paintings by female artists, we heard 10 women read their work to an audience ranging in age between seven and 80 years. Through the evening's expressions of a fraction of the silent majority, we embraced the strength and determination within our power as women.

Within the context of Vincentian life at the time, *Seen and Heard* was an unusual gathering in two ways. Firstly, those present discovered the relationships between the visual and verbal art forms, and secondly, through its content, they learned of the creative and graphic articulation of the lives and concerns of the silent majority of women.

Each visual and literary artwork in the *Seen and Heard* forum was based on acute internal observation, and whilst expressing personal experiences, articulated the universal voice of women. The artists inspired all who heard their words and saw their images not only to express themselves but to have hope in the positive energy rarely seen or heard in our communities. These voices came together with a determination that made grown men in the audience shed tears as they recognised the unspoken voice of their mothers, the spiritual strength and unity of women communicating the resilience, love and compassion, the defiance, the strength and humility that have preserved and revitalised our spirits throughout our challenging history.

These ideas and thoughts of women form a critical foundation of cohesive social relationships that are desperately needed to emerge more forcefully to develop and heal our wounded communities.

Many on our islands may be skeptical or dismissive of creativity addressing pressing social problems, negative behaviour and attitudes, but I have seen creative action transform the lives of many young people through being given the tools, guidance and enabling environment to express their own thoughts through words, through images, through movement and music, through community action.

That evening we felt the healing and unifying power of women's creativity.

The Ambassador, Yoel Pérez Marcano, was so moved by what he saw and heard, that he immediately offered assistance through the Embassy of the Bolivarian Republic of Venezuela to publish a collection of our works.

And so this anthology appropriately came into being through a process of engagement: the birthing of collective creative life that we hope will spread to resonate through the lives of those who it touches. All involved in its creation hope that we will no longer feel alone and frightened in the knowledge that we can accomplish greater things together and bring our communities to the positive cultural and spiritual entities that they can be.

We heartily thank Ambassador Yoel Pérez Marcano and his staff at the Embassy of the Bolivarian Republic of Venezuela for their invaluable support and assistance in validating our aesthetic expressions through the production of this, the first anthology of creations of Vincentian women poets and visual artists.

Vonnie Roudette
Penniston, St. Vincent

Reckoning Woman Poet

(For Thunder and Shake)

I is a…
I ain't no…
I is a…
I ain't no…
I is a…
I don't know…
I am
waiting for a signal…

They call me,
left over,
the Biblical spare, the sidekick,
submissive, never main,
second made, don't complain,
elevated prostitute – somebody's wife,
body bludgeoned between
dichotomies of the
Madonna-Whore type,
still not quite
satisfying
corporeal parameters,
taxing standards,

shrink wrapped in
banners cutting circulation
cutting circulation
cutting circulation
banners shrunk tight
asphyxia imposed;
totally covered – empress,
skin exposed – temptress,
if either gets raped,
blame finds a familiar space,
"It's your fault you know,
walking tit and ass fest that you are,
God made you beautiful,
God made you beautiful by far...."
I is a...
I ain't no...
I is a...
I ain't no...
I is a...
I don't know...
I am
waiting for a symbol...

Mother bought me nothing
but books, Alice in wonderland
through looking glass books,
had me hooked from early
me and them books
became best friends
became best friends
me and them books
became best friends,
then
I thought I could write books
and when I went to write books
what greeted me was
masculinity,

slapped with
penis envy,
anxious for authorship,
anxious for authorship
looking like me.
Wrote a poem about it,
spoke some prose about it,
got chucked into therapy
psychoanalytical reject,
conditioned to live
nervous perpetually,
'cause the fat ass, huge tits
and white masks don't fit.
Shit,
how do I
patch this rift?
How do I
find a salve that's
legit?
How do I find the
the ointment for atonement,
the anointment for this
thousand year headache?

I is a...
I ain't no...
I is a...
I ain't no...
I is a...
I don't know...
I am
waiting...

I flipped
this mania,
I flipped this mania,
I flipped this mania

and joined the ranks of
the creatively schizophrenic,
I flipped this mania
and joined the ranks of
the creatively schizophrenic:
manic ascending,
manic obsessive,
manic redemptive,
manic replenished,
manic prophetic,
manic sophisti-
cated, and sending
love through your
mind,
love through your
mind
stimulating that
pineal gland,
that third eye
opening to
chakra heights,
third eye.

I is a
POET
I is a
WOMAN
POET
I is a
POET WOMAN
It's done,
now I
know it.

I is a
POET
I is a

WOMAN
POET
I is a
POET WOMAN
It's done,
now you
know it.

—*Debra Providence*

OUR JOURNEY

Wombleaf, Natana McLean
oil pastel

This image in oil and chalk pastel embodies the journey of growth and beauty, strength and process of an ordinary leaf. It honours the miracle of what is around us – like the energy of women everywhere, its power often goes unnoticed.

Black Sea Memoirs of an African Slave Girl

Sea blue, sea white, sea black
over we go with no turning back
chains on our hands, feet and neck
crumbled
together below the deck
rocking in motion from left to right
when will we see the promising light
mama, papa, brother all here
one square corner we all got to share

Oh I remember back home back there
back when everything was simple and fair
when skies were clear, though lands were bare
we sit, we sing, we laugh, we share

Room dark like tar, how hungry we are
floor sticky and wet, air hot from sweat
can't move, can't stand, can't wait to reach land

To look at the man who shackled our hands,
to look in his eyes try uncover his plans
for bringing we blacks over to this land

To land we came tired and unfree
the man he came bearing a key
with pain in our hearts we wondered what would be
after coming so far over this black sea

–Janeele Jackson

Warigabaga[1]

While Garinagu[2]
Reflected on
Struggle in
Yurumein
And looming
Loss of language
Warigabaga
Sped gracefully in –

Warigabaga
Child of the day
Awakened from sleep
Avoided the light and settled
Delicately authoritatively
On the DRUM!
The ancestors had come
To counsel!

II
Garinagu break forth
From your cocoon!
You holders of the
Knowledge

Let it fly free
As Warigabaga!

III
Warigabaga is a coat
Of many colors
Versatile
Multiplied hope
The spirit of Garifunaduau

Warigabaga is life
Awakened
Answering the heart beat
Drum beat!

Garinagu!
Sing and drum
That your fire
May blaze
Dance the dance
Of life
Sing and drum
That your fire may blaze
Dance! Like
Warigabaga!

—Nelcia Robinson Hazell

[1]Warigabaga – Butterfly
[2]Garinagu – A race of indigenous people or Black Caribs

My Caribbean

My Caribbean
What month
Were you born?
Beautiful child
Of the sun

Cradling a friendly sea
Crowded by land masses
Whose motherhood
Makes you jump and sing
Or whose shadows
Cause you to crawl

My Caribbean
Peopled by many races
Exploited by the Church
And royalty
Whose purple and cruel greed
Made martyrs of my Carib ancestry
And slaves of my African sisters and brothers

My Caribbean
inheritor of the disease
Of dependency
And bruised youth
Possessor of the
Spirit of resistance
Building national
And regional organizations
Saying a decisive "No"
To cultural invasion

My Caribbean
Beauty and rugged strength
Today is your birthday
As you are delivered
From your pot-shaped womb
And claim the resources
Of peoples, land and sea
Holding high your placards of
Adult education – Mass Education
A Political Statement of Change!

–Nelcia Robinson Hazell

Chatoyer's Children

In a little village
Close by a friendly sea
The years rolled back
And like faces on a canvas
I saw Chatoyer's children

Bright and eager
They questioned me
Was I Garifuna people too
Then how come
I could not speak Garifuna?
Why?

And I told them
I am of the Garinagu in Yurumein
But lack of use
Persecution
And foreign influence
Swallowed up our language
And covered some of our culture
But in our genes
We are Chatoyer's children

Then they nodded wisely
Knowing that from the cradle
They are taught
About the ancestors
And Yurumein land –
So, where was it?
What do the people eat?
What is the national animal?

So I forgot the sadness
Of my loss
And in lisping, laughing voice
Told them of the bananas
And arrowroot, cassava
Yams, tannias, eddoes
And dasheen

Like a bubbling river
My voice flowed on
To speak of the
133 square miles of
Beautiful mountainous
Volcanic Yurumein
18 miles long by 11 miles wide
And the 17 square miles
Necklace of 32 islands and cays
The lovely Grenadines

The parrot Vincie
Our national bird
Flies free above
The green, gold and
Blue of our flag – the gems
Colorful and unique
Alongside the Soufriere tree –
Our national flower
And blessing the national dish

Roast breadfruit and
Fried Jack fish

The Coat of Arms
Cries out for peace
And justice
In a Caribbean land
Where 113 thousand
Hardworking people
Honor the Paramount Chief
Of our ancestors
And are become
Chatoyer's children

Then they nodded wisely
And I heard them resolve
We will keep our culture
We will pass it on
To our relatives
In Yurumein
And in Hopkins Village
There will always be Chatoyer's children

–Nelcia Robinson Hazell

Sweet Cruelty

With fiery iron rods
It ruled the day
In all its glory
   It saturated the
   Atmosphere with
   Unbearable heat
   There was a sense of mercilessness in the air
As it danced across the sky in cruel glee
(but the day was magnificent)
As it watched the little humans
Scurrying about under umbrellas
Fainting and absorbing liquids like sponges
In its explosive 'hot dance'
Time was pushing it right to the western sky
Where it turned to a huge, beautiful
Delicious orange ball of Mello cream butter
As the multi-hued clouds gently pat it to sleep

–*Jecinta Hope Knights*

De Racket Bar

Me want fo open Racket Bar
Me hear it mek harddough,
But Veeny say me ha fo tes'
De feasibility

Me ain't no marketin' expert,
Me ain't pass mats nor stats
Me can't afford consultants' fee
Me poor like parson mice

So me go ha fo use me eye
Fo do market survey
'Cause sense mek before book conceive
De small man glad fo dat
No overheads, jis underheads,
No income tax returns
No big signpos' fo draw de crowd
Jis crookedness an' tact

Me tink ganga is starting pint,
Me leeward frien' dream so.

An' den me could diversify
Wid cocaine an' de res'
Me can't lef' out de contraban'
An' bootliquor from cays,
An' den me operate Queen Show
In stocious racket style

De sidewalk games don't intris me
But U.S. Visa do,
Me tink me better check Tall Boy
Fo get legal advice

Me wish me fine one Spanish Jar!
Me woulda buy Youlou,
'Cause dem ole people hoard nuff bread
Fo mek orwee live high

De police can't ketch-up wid me
'Cause fo me little trade
Does retail fo de M.I.A.,
An' dem big man don't joke

Darlin', dis is a crooked worl'.
An' if you don't conform
You boun' fo en' up a' poor home
An' Bun Pan res' yo soul

                                    —Joyce Peters McKenzie

Home Not Home

Misplaced, mismatched
Newly lost, newly hatched
Home not home

Homing birds
Come finding an abandoned roost
Disorientated from long flights
South and North
My fragmented voice
Registers the flight path
Vowels unsteady
Crashing through overgrown neural pathways
To a word under used

Misused, misplaced
Newly minted sounds outta place
Out of place not outta place
Somehow the name don't fit dem face
Not dem but those the ones who speak
The childhood voices but a bat squeak
To warn of dangerous currents
in landing home not home

–Clare Ibberson-John

Black People

Show them
Show them your feet, your hands, your eyes
Show them the tears that stream from your cries
Show them your hurt, your love, your pain
Show them your heart, your soul, your gain
Show them that life can be obtained, sustained and maintained
in this life of oppression, we've all been contained
   to live in and grow in
but now we must refrain, and show them our reign
   just as it was before they came.
Show them your talents, your color, your name
Show them your culture for they've stolen your fame
Show them your mind, your wit, your skills
Show then you're more than just stacking up bills
Show them your light, your sight, your might
Show them that life is worth the fight
Show them the love that runs within
Show them,
Show them again.

—Janeele Jackson

Rolling Water

From her four corners
Pachamama
Has sent forth her daughters
Beautiful and strong
Survivors of yesterday
Laden with the heat
And burden of today

Touch her now
The sister by your side
Feel the pain
Below the joy
Show her the light above
The darkness
Touch her now
The sister in that corner

Listen to her now
The sister from Africa
Hear the message
Spoken without words
Does it come as Rolling Water
A vibrant sound of life
Or hopelessness

As wind in dry grass?
Listen to her now
The Asian sister
Weep with her now
The sister from Latin America

From the four corners
Of the Pachamama
You the healers have come
To strengthen the hands
Of the sister from Europe
And bind the wounds
Of your Caribbean sister

But the moment is fleeting
After today
How can you hold her
The sister from the Pacific
Reach the North American sister

Speak to her now
The sister by your side
Knit a living net
And walk within
To the sister
In that corner
Life will spring
From the ashes

For under it is
Pachamama

Walk with her now
The sister by your side
Walk with her now,
The sister in that corner

        –Nelcia Robinson Hazell

OURSELVES

gullee goddess go wid Jah, "booops"
acrylic paint on board

In "gullee goddess", an image taken from a life drawing "booops" did at art school in Jamaica is awakened into a collage of surfaces. "It conjures up a colleck-shun of emotions dat (h)onher d eva lasting endurance of woman....at one time we all find ourself 'pan pause', stripped bare, longing tooo RISE agen....."

Enlightenment

I saw you today
and my fear of not being able to look away
is making me take quick glances
at the lines of your face and the curve of your smile,
eyes twinkling like city lights in the dead of night as you spoke
passionately about God knows what

But that's how you got when you were affected by something

Like when you told me about the prisoners in Cuba
and your intent to help free them

Or the land of your birth, a place so beautifully
stricken with poverty that it carved pain on the faces
of the millions who lived there

I remember listening to you
My head nesting in the curve of your shoulder, pressing my nose
into your chest inhaling your scent and absorbing
every
word
spoken

Feeling them rain down on me as you pulled me into your thoughts
and held me there, cradled between what once was, what is,

what will be
Showing me your passions the way a parent teaches a child his ABC's, patiently
Allowing me to trip, fall, stumble over your words as I sprint
to catch up with your dreams

You were always a dreamer

Dreaming as you guided me away from the child I was and
introducing me to the woman I was meant to be
Hand in hand we stood, fingers grasping, palms touching,
handshake firm as we acknowledged each other

I, blushing, meeting this person for the first time
touching my face, fixing my hair, amazed by her and
she looks at me in amazement, seeing in me the girl
that she once was, the girl she would no longer be
having lost her innocence on life's journey a long time ago

So lost was she in me and I in her that we both seemed to forget
that you were there
Until time spoke
Ever of the essence

One step forward with the other foot behind the line
Too afraid to move

And I, taking quick glances at the child I used to be gaze back
at the woman
I've become and
I love her

Love her the way a mother would love a child ceaselessly,
selflessly and without judgment
Watching the pieces fall in place like a puzzle already figured out

This is what I was made for.

—Jeneille Lewis

Young Woman

Young Woman, fragile shoot
I am afraid for you
You are so vulnerable

Young Woman, tender vine
I am afraid for you
You are denied guidance

Young Woman, slender leafy plant
I am afraid for you
You are so innocent
Glorying in the discovery
Of your beauty

Young Woman, blossoming palm tree
You are on the threshold
Of life in all its fullness
I am afraid for you
You are exposed to the elements
Of violence, disillusion and
Discrimination

Fruits of an unjust social and
Economic arrangement

Young woman
Be a sealed fountain
In an enclosed garden
Whose walls are to be scaled
When you are woman,
Conscious, positive
Goal setting
Confident woman

Young Woman, be wise
Guard your dignity
Acknowledge your
Potential
Father, Mother
Older Man, Older Woman
Uncle, Aunt, Brother, Sister

Young Woman
Be a hedge around her
Bruise not the flower

−Nelcia Robinson Hazell

A Bad Example of a Lady

When we were young and yet beribboned
11 or 12 or so
We filed into high school classrooms
To learn what we should know
Our teachers all assured us
Once the transformation was complete
We'd be the epitome of ladies
Dignified and sweet
With childish enthusiasm we assiduously took note
Of the strictest education in "stop", "never" and "don't":

Don't thump or walk ungracefully

Lightly place heel before the toe.

Tuck the bottom, square the shoulders, lift the chin.

Don't sag at the knees, but don't lock them.

Turn on the toe and pivot your body, gently unwrapping
    to the new direction you're going in.

Never offer your hand to a man.

Stand far enough away that you can't be touched.

Don't be too familiar with the guys.

Keep your knees together when you sit, cross your legs at the ankle.

Remember only slatterns expose their thighs.

Smile, but don't show too much teeth.

You may chuckle if something is funny, but too loud of a laugh
    is vulgar and uncouth.
Relax your face and hold in your stomach.

For heaven's sake hold in your stomach if you want to keep
    the figure of your youth.

Nothing is more déclassé than swishing your ass.

Never sway when you walk.

You must look respectable when you pass – you know how
    people like to talk!

Remember – you're a lady. No raucousness and yelling.

Don't speak loudly, instead let your lips form your words
    before gently expelling.

Don't overly gesticulate, or wave your hands about. It's coarse
    behavior and besides you don't want to be mistaken
    for some common layabout.

Red shoes are tartish as are ankle bracelets.
    (Prostitutes wear those you know!)

Never ever drink straight from a bottle. (Why? Because
  I told you so!)

Stop popping that gum! Spit it out!

Now, put your right foot forward, balance gracefully.

Knees together. Knees together! We wouldn't want to be
  that kind of lady, now would we?

But see –
No matter how many times I posed the question
None of my teachers had a lesson
That would clearly make me see
What being a lady would do for me
Everything based on future self or something I was doing
  for someone else
Just be polite and quiet – act like everything's fine
And when the meek inherit the earth I'll be one of the first in line?
Well excuse me if that ain't convincing
when men are getting theirs all the time
I don't want to be seen someday, I want my spotlight now
I should be able to be myself without having to bow
Down to a set of made up rules
Or climb up on a pedestal
It's too easy to fall when all
Some people want is a caricature
A myth – an idealized self I'm forced to observe
Why should I knock off my rough edges
just to better accommodate yours?

If you think I'm unladylike now, why not try this on for size
I'll be inappropriate, uncooperative and radical 'til I die
Fi mi mout nah jine no chuch
I'll give you back chat till you're sick
won't sacrifice my rights for peace – this is my voice and my lips

Since being sweet will not protect me from the scorn
   of certain "ladies"
Who ironically join with every other force that's out to play me
Because my choices are incongruent with what they imagine
   a lady to be
I didn't find a man in college and
Maybe marriage ain't for me
I cradle my ambitions – they're like children to me
For the men I know who constantly want to put me in a box
Looking at my sexual history to judge what I am and
   what I'm not
Screw you
Really
I can say this to you freely
That who I choose to sleep with is completely my affair
And if you're stupid enough to take the conversation there
You best be prepared
For a fight, 'cause see
I've had it up to here with Madonna-whore dichotomies
I'm frigid if I don't give it up, I'm a whore if I do
So I'm gon' do what works for me with someone who ain't you.

But like Nina Simone please don't let me be misunderstood
I'm not a rebel without a cause, just spouting off because I could
I have a right to be hostile
Not hysterical or passive aggressive
Or other female connoted adjective
Designed to downplay my stress
Like some kind of tantrum or PMS
I just want to be equal – nothing more, nothing less
It's not my job to make it simple
Present myself for mass consumption
You want me to define myself
So you can determine a position
From which to attack me
But I'm determined not to afford you the opportunity
To use your fear to try to pin me down with false binaries.

I'm not an idea, I'm a person
Not magician or contortionist
There's no amount of twisting that will make this square peg fit
But I'm proud to be used as a bad example of a lady
A sign of things to come and the hope that someday maybe
We can all be seen as women
Three-dimensional and flawed
Multifaceted and complex
Free to let it all hang out
And while I sip beers from the bottle
  I'll be sure to stick my pinky out.

−Alisa Alvis

His Sonnet (Cereal Box Love)

You got me thinking happy thoughts
Like sunny and bubbly and children laughing thoughts
Like happiness is now beginning and loneliness is ending thoughts
Like you were meant for me and I was meant for you
and on this we both agree
And you and me and this and we should have happened before
'Cause you and her never worked together
and me and him
Should have been together
But you and me, we can see forever
Like circular movement on a merry-go-round
And my laughter is like a never ending song
Like gypsies covering my heartache with joy
And I walk around singing "I'm in love with a boy"
When you look at me I get lost in your dream
That you spin and weave and stuff full of truths that you mean
See when you look at me I see my reflection in your eyes
And in her eyes I see yours so full of surprise

Like contentment was a thing you've never known
And this love was a thing you've never been shown

And happy is this feeling that I feel when you're around

Like a little child playing with a favorite toy that he found

Like finding that toy at the bottom of a cereal box
The kind where you never check how many calories
the cereal's got
Like
Lucky Charms and Honey Nut Cheerios
And
Butterfly kisses sprinkled on the bridge of my nose
Like
Hershey's Kisses in the center of my bed
Tiny hearts replacing sheets soiled with remorse and regret
Like
The way you look at me like I'm the only girl in the room
And the way you close your eyes when you inhale my perfume
See I could go on and on about you and me
But the only thing that matters is you make me happy

–Jeneille Lewis

6:17

Six minutes, seventeen seconds
I listen to you in your absence
Believing everything that you say in that moment
In this element you are the most honest that you will ever be
In this moment
Six minutes
Seventeen seconds
You are real and without fault
Perfection
You cannot lie
Not by admission
Not by omission
In this medium that you command
You are vulnerable and raw
And you cannot disguise the angle of your intent
You cannot prevent the revelation of your soul
Six minutes
Seventeen seconds
Before you go
And I awake

–Jeneille Lewis

Crescendo (flip-side of 6:17)

The way my heart beats when I get excited
This pitter-pattering of pulses that runs and skips and trips
   and hops and explodes
Like fire
I want to rip at my flesh so that I can open my chest and
   bare my soul
Show you the light that glows
This love, this trust, this peace, this truth
I want to run, not away from but to as I feel the oxygen
   surging through my veins and lifting me higher
This urgency to be, to soar, to live
This ceaseless flow of passion that has nothing to do with sex
This release as it finds its way from my heart, to my soul,
   to my hand, to this page
To your eyes
To your mind
Feel me touch you
Caress you with my words and provoke your thoughts with
   the imagery that I present
I am before you, naked
Vulnerable

Asking you to see me for what I am
To take me as I am
To love me in spite of my flaws and my inadequacies in a craft
  that I am trying to master
I write for you, honestly
Hoping that my words are sufficient
Because I will always be honest with them
Written or
Spoken
I have never lied to you

–Jeneille Lewis

I Don't Think I'm Ever Satisfied

It's all happening so fast,
The feelings gone into overdrive, in the space of a minute
I KNOW YOU
In the space of three you know me
And more...
Where to touch, where to take your time
It's no mystery anymore because now I'll play your game.
Butterflies are eating the lonely out my stomach filling it with over
joy
Everything's over capacity when I'm with you
But when I'm with him memories of how I felt come back
A kiss never to be regretted, a taste never to be forgotten,
A stare never to be set on anyone else but me.
I don't care anymore if my mind is playing tricks
This state called ecstasy; mere bliss?
Ma fires ignite, ma soul burns from its flames
Am I in hell for ma sins? Did I do wrong?

He looks at me I'm filled.
I smile but he looked away...
I was quick to put myself at fault

He calls ma name; I run to him
Yet he has absolutely nothing to say.
I am confused
Speak to me dammit!
I've waited,
Heaven knows it has been way too long
This time tell him wait
Tell them both to wait
Draw the curtain; I will not do this nude scene 'til the bruises are gone
They'll go away right?
Scars left, no amount of makeup could cover
HE sees right through me.
The other questions, but he smiles in memory
The other loves, but he lusts for my body
One is beyond me, the other is creeping to my level

I want to be held and grabbed at the same time
Kissed and bitten
Caressed and slapped
Spoilt and neglected
Listened to and ignored
Comforted and hurt

Can I have you both?
Because I don't think I'm ever really satisfied!

                              —Felicia Gabrielle George

Journey to Isolation, Narissa Ballantyne
oil paint

In this painting there are two centres: one light, the other dark. The dark centre has light coming from it; the light one radiates darkness, symbolising confusion I feel hiding in the world. Even behind the brightest of colours is a dark story. The eyes reflect the soul hungering for creativity and thirsting for knowledge. Feeling unwanted by society, I found my own world through the journey of creating this painting.

It Was Beautiful,
and Then Came the Storm

The storm comes only when they're near
Insecurities like the wind
Come blowing in
Messing up my hair...
I had combed it so neat (it was beautiful)
Now in my mind I search for a brush
My hand is my friend, he fixes my hair.

The storm comes only when she's near
Tears like the rain
Come flooding in
Soaking my paper...
I once had hopes and dreams (it was beautiful)
Now in my mind I search for pen and paper
My friends, they dry my tears.

The storm comes only when he's near
Heartbeats like the thunder
Come crashing in
Drowning my voice...

I cannot sing like before (it was beautiful)
Now I'm in search of my voice
To speak, to sing, my friend finds it
You lead the way.

The storm comes only when I'm near
Insecurities, tears, heartbeats, and doubt like the lightning
Come flashing in
Revealing my truth – for that split second
I can achieve and leave my mark
I saw it I can sing and speak (it was beautiful)
Now in my mind I have a light, my friend...
Let me see beauty though the storm blocks my path.

                                        –Felicia Gabrielle George

Prediction

I hate you.

you predicted this
like everything else you predicted my emotion at the end of it all
you told me I'd despise you
you told me this whilst breathing honey-dipped words into my ear

I hate you

you told me that I would
you insisted I would as you spread your sweet venom down my thighs
whispered this to me as I moaned my reluctance to let you go
you gripped me, held me, pulling me closer
Letting me go

I hate you

the way you made me feel
before we...
during...
after the storm had ceased and you were gone
I hate you

not because you left me

but because you should have

left
me
alone
before I knew what it was like to have you
to hold you
to breathe the air when you were gone and still find you there...

I loved you

before I knew I could
before I knew I would
before you even touched me
before you showed me that it was possible to be like you
to be just
like
you

I loved you until I started hating you
and now I hate everything about you

every word you speak

every lie you feel necessary to tell

I hate this memory

this air that I breathe that refuses to let the smell of you go

I hate you

I don't love you

I hate you

                         —Jeneille Lewis

Seeing Eyes

Come me Child
God bless yo
A see a fan
Fanning yo
Fanning yo
God bless yo
Me Chile

Yo does help people
Plenty nuh?
Yo does give way
Money ah ting
Yes! Yes!
Keep it up Chile
Yo bread basket
Will never empty
Yo cup will full
To the brim
An run over

But look!
A man dark face
Over yo shoulder
Look him dey
Over yo lef shoulder
Yes Chile

A don't know
If is fo good
Or bad,
But pray, Chile
Pray
Dat yo get a good
Companion
One who will be a father to yo

So yo going now
God bless yo
Me Chile
Keep up yo
Good work
Come kiss me
Leh me feel yo
But like yo drawing!
Ah! Me Chile
Yo does wuk hard...
Yo see dat malt
Mix it wid some milk an a egg
And drink it
It will build yo
Stomach
Yes, me Chile
Do what I tell yo now
It wiii buiid yo stomach

May de Lord
Go wid yo
If we neva see
One another
Face again
May we meet over yonda
God bless yo me Chile
God go wid yo, Me Chile....

        –Nelcia Robinson Hazell

Beauty

beauty is you
beauty is me
beauty is humble
beauty is free!
we frown, we smile, we stare, we look
upon our sisters with condescending hooks,
you see i'm guilty and maybe you are the same
of judging your sisters without even knowing their names
liking, hating, judging what we see
not knowing one bit about how it came to be
why do we do that, is it to keep our own self
image intact?
to think, oh wow she looks nice or look at her!
   i wonder what's the price?
we look at their shapes, comment on their hair
and talk about what they should or should not wear
but beauty is love, hope and faith
beauty was given so that we all can create all that is good, it's not
hard to see, that beauty is in you and beauty is in me.

–Janeele Jackson

Re-entry Blues

I wandered lonely as a cloud
That floats on high o'er vales and hills
When no warning given, shot down mid-flight
With a resounding "serves you right"
You silly little bitch to think at all
That you could fly, we'll see you fall
Crashing through a green canopy deceptively thorned
The saving branches of the arms of friends were armed
Not strong to catch but dead and hollow rotting sticks
Withered, diseased from lack of care and pruning
These trees not destined to withstand
Any sudden increased demand

Yes, off you fly but don't come back
To land with flightless grumbling fowl
Whose only life is pecking the grit of misfortunes
To help digest their caged bird life
While sitting in wait and unaware
That while they nested
Was a world
Out there

Pecking at martyred stay-at-home wounds
Pecking at mistreatment wrongly assumed
Picking at phantom fears and slights
Clipping their own wings of dangerous flight
Yes, off you fly but don't come back
Reminding us that at least you went
And strayed off track
Lost and lonely
Wandering loose
While we waited
Caged
Necks
Noosed

–Clare Ibberson-John

Hidden Fears Rise in Hope, Shanelle Bascombe
acrylic oil pastel and paper collage

This image came from a long process of development from self-portrait
drawings. The hands symbolise both reaching out and holding back
because of inner confusion. The inner face is the one within that holds a
lot of fear. The open eye symbolises hope, the closed eye, disappointment.
Light shows the transformation of consciousness from awareness. It's an
optimistic resolution, full of hope.

Phoenix Rising

Grey dust stirs
as her feet leave
fiery prints
in a well-scorched earth;
weed and orchid
insect and bird
frozen in their last
terrified gasp,
ashen,
they crumble
before her stare.

Behind her:
the world is
sucked dry;
in front:
none will escape
the glare of
crimson death.

Inside:
caged, bleeding,
a redbreast,

fluttering frantically,
balance thrown
by a broken wing
pierced by
a poisoned
iron tip...
her song
is taken,
in its place
a shrill wail
shatters
unwary ears.
She,
once burned,
rises to
sear
a stale, flat
and wicked
Earth.

–*Debra Providence*

Silent Love

You loved me in my youth
I wished you away
Years passed
Your life returned in silent truth

–Jecinta Hope Knights

Forest River Moon

In the flowing river all things are possible:
the breath of thought; mountain might.
As our reflection slips away,
forest river remains
millennia steadfast.

But then an interference
in the last second
of their existence
diminished rivers cry thirst
as human charges uproot their source.

Great gifted humans,
recede on the banks
of living community purpose
to be managed in glorified artifices
that line walls and corridors.
But the powerful river
calls back her precious charges
and unifies those who
move like river think like water.

The source is replenished
by itself.

                                        −Vonnie Roudette

Sea Water Moon

The ocean weeps her immense
body of wisdom upon our shores with glistening tears
    shed
for vanishing memories.
She rises up and swells with grief
            that mourns the loss of our connection

She has watched her coastline
manipulated into the hostile partner she lies with

She no longer recognises
her body contours,
pleading the overseeing moon and sky

"Mother is calling"
is the message
in each mournful wave
that breaks unheard against
our altered shores.

                                        –Vonnie Roudette

The Call of Nature

Sitting on my bed, feeling waves of slow depressing energy
  flowing over
my body, I try to stand, I try to move my hand, my feet,
  nothing won't
budge. I breathe in what could be my last breath,
  my limbs feel like
the weight of many pulling me down to my demise.
  I open my eyes, hoping
that this will free me, but alas it brings me even deeper
  into my
Despair
I hear sounds of nature outside my window,
  I can hear the deafening
sound of the rain pounding against the roof.
  I feel like I'm being
pierced by the very action of those rain drops,
  my heart explodes for
wanting to be free! My mind goes blank from the emptiness
I feel
inside, I feel nothing!
The force of the wind ignores my plea and rushes
  against my window,

bringing with it the cold entity that is its breath. I sink into my pillow, I turn my head trying to block its penetration into my soul. It's getting stronger, I can feel its power, its energy surrounding me! It takes over me, I'm its own forever.

The bright light beams into my room, its rays of gold and fire blind my sight. I open my eyes, it's morning. It's over. It's done. But I feel different...I'm not the same, I've been changed. My being has been raped with the essense of Nature. I'm one with her.
  I am Nature.

–Janeele Jackson

OUR WORLD

Emotional Contortions, Shonette Bynoe
acrylic, oil pastel

This started as drawings of a plastic bag stuffed full, hanging on a door handle that I used as an allegory to represent a host of emotional problems about to burst. As I explored through drawing, I noticed sequences of movements and rhythms created by light changes over the surface. The drawings evolved, reminding me of scales in music, of beautiful harmonies and rhythms. I began to try to find the brighter side of life and my problems were then symbolically transformed into "melodies of life".

To the Men

Your women of virtue, your women of pride
your women of class standing at your side.
Oh how she glows with life all around
saying so much without making a sound.
Love her, respect her, attend to her needs;
trust her, pamper her, make it your creed.
Listen when she talks, admire her when she walks,
be with her in every way, be with her day by day,
let her know you're here to stay.
Wash for her, clean for her, help her with dinner;
massage her back, wash her feet,
you never know you might get a treat.
Let not your minds be corrupted with old tales
that women should not do the same as males.
Encourage her in whatever she may want to pursue
for love of your woman is pure and true.
Women are wise, courageous and strong;
women are lovely, ambitious and almost never wrong.
So love your woman with heart and conviction,
love your woman with dreams and visions,
love your woman with everything you've got,
love your woman, love her a lot.

–Jeneele Jackson

Before You Ask

Yes that's my daughter
No she's not adopted
Yes her daddy is dark
No he's not Indian
Yes he's black
No he's not from Jamaica
Yes it's in the Caribbean
No you've never heard of it
Yes we are married
No I wasn't on holiday
Yes I knew him a long time before that
No we've been together for 17 years
Yes he's got a British passport
No he had one before we met
Yes my parents like him a lot
No they came to the wedding
Yes that's all his hair
No he's not cut it since 1972
Yes he washes it
No you can't grow yours like that

Yes he takes his hat off in bed
No it doesn't get in the way

Yes I love him
No I'm not into black men
Yes he's hot
No it's not that big
Yes people always ask me that
No I'm sure you didn't mean anything by it
Yes I'm sick of your questions
No I'm not being rude
Yes I'm upset
No don't apologise
Yes I'm telling my husband
And before you ask
Yes you should be worried

–Clare Ibberson-John

Forget You Had a Father

Forget you had a father
Forget that he only shook your hand
And left for 14 years while you became man
Forget he made your heart stone hard
Nah tek one piece of chicken
Two cock can't live in one yard

Forget that your mother left for the cold
And called for your pretty sister
Forget that you were left to struggle
And you pretended that you nah miss 'er

Forget that you are a stubborn pig man
Forget that you can't be ruled
Forget that you hurt us
and forget that we won't forgive you

Remember that when they grow up
They won't always remember
That your life was tough, you weren't loved enough
Your hurt was not healed
So remember

                    —Clare Ibberson-John

True Reflections, Nerissa King
acrylic paint, oil pastel

This image emerged from drawings of reflections of myself. As I proceeded to develop the images, many facets of myself emerged, and I learned about how we women are full of ideas and creativity. My perception of myself expanded through these visual manifestations that have universal meaning about women's strength and endurance.

Platanal Lullaby

Go to sleep! Go to sleep, my dear
Safe within the sandman's care
He will gently take your hand
Lead you to a happy land

There you'll dream, dream of bottled milk,
And of puppies dressed in coats of silk
You shall also see goats of pedigree,
And a cocker-doodle-do who won't crow to startle you

Donkeys grey, chicks in fine array,
All in grand parade, by the sandman made
Rattles, teddy bears, bunnies with long ears,
The kind sandman will show
To babes who with him go

Flags and gay balloons, sun and stars and moon,
Endless things to suck, only dreams can bring such luck
Do not fight, surrender to his might
In the sandman's arms, share those dreamland charms

Cease your peevish cries,
Close your little eyes
The sandman knows what's best
Babies must have rest

Go to sleep! Go to sleep my dear,
Safe within the sandman's care
He will gently take your hand

                              −Nora Peacock

Parents on Parade
(Common Entrance Remix)

A quiet room of uncertain faces
Waiting to be put through their parents' paces
Turning fans the only sound
Traffic noise turned down
Normal volume in Kingstown
Strangely mute
I sit wearing my best-foot-forward suit

Oh innocent foolish new recruit
Drafting your children to pointless pursuits
Tested and drilled, automatic response
Multiple choice with no choice of expression
Beaten with Stingah and no chance of escape
Prepared to go over the top in one last push
To compete for more of the same
No sah, no sah, not in my name
Name, rank and number
Seared in their brains
Your army is unthinking, our children defeated

Soldiers prepared for a battle not needed,
Attrition of intellect
War on the masses
Sergeant we are missing
We're bunning your classes
AWOL
Absconding
Gone clear

                    —Clare Ibberson-John

Little Woman

her shadow stretches
six feet in front of her
much like her future
it is ahead of her
but it is
dark, distorted,
insubstantial, unavoidable
and hers alone to endure
like the other little women
she is uniformed
in her tight jeans
revealing her over-developed frame
those child bearing hips
deceive the onlooker
into believing
that her mind is ready
for what her body can produce and chances are
she's lost her chance
years ago
chances to a positive role model
the only roles

she models are those
of the half-naked dancers
in those music videos
those songs little woman knows
by heart
she mouths the words
believing those misogynists
who call her explicit names
and she agrees that she
deserves it
little woman sucks her thumb
doesn't speak like a woman
can't read like a woman
lacks the confidence of a woman
she is biologically mature
and mentally premature for
her child
who sits in the stroller
beside her
on a day
when little woman should be in school

–Jamillah Burgin

War Poppies

Fields of poppies,
A generation of army boys
Blanketed minds by history books.
My prayer for their rest.

–Jecinta Hope Knights

She Finds Herself

She finds herself
in this situation
again
except this time
she knows
what will happen and
she knows
she'll regret it

> *–Jamillah Burgin*

Unworthy Lifestyle

Hot angry tears streamed down her face
She swore she wouldn't let him do this to her again,
Not like this
She became so vulnerable in his arms again
Let the trust grow back to what it was
"Do it once, blame's on you
Do it twice, the blame's on me"
It was she who covered herself in shame
She wasn't supposed to get so close
She had all the reasons, the years of pain,
And those numerous floodings of tears
She had the scars to show
The verbal blows her heart and mind know
She has become weak and susceptible in his eyes again
He takes advantage and lashes out
She has done no wrong but is still punished
Punished for wanting to be loved
Needing love…
He was the last person who said "I love you" to her
Maybe she wanted this, people say

But she doesn't
She cries out for help with her heart
No one can hear and those who can
They simply refuse to listen
She has done no wrong but he still lashes out...

–Felicia Gabrielle George

My Other Life

He wore our secret
like a stolen garment
and curled into its
quiet moments when
angry stares swirled
cold around me

I trapped your touch
inside
and waited
like a fugitive
until the cruel hours
tripped
on the edge of dawn
and tumbled into
silence

Then I'd unleash my
memories of you
and dare to smile
as they lift me
eagerly
into another day
where you wait with
my other life
stored safely in your
eyes

—*Peggy Carr*

Prayer for Prosperity, Amanda Frederick
paper collage, acrylic paint

This image collates the various strengths of the matriarch through a patchwork
of collage textures, filling the praying hands and arms of her grandmother.
Woman as moral strength, as guide and as provider is the message as the
interlocking fingers hold firm our collective spiritual heritage.

Scorpio Descending

Scorpio descends,
squatting on a rusted
moral pillar,
stomach stuffed and distended
with narcissus pies.
Blunted stinger misses
mark that blind Scorpio will
not see, and while Scorpio sleeps
the macrocosm still
burns along its orbit.
The periphery has shifted
considerably beyond
peripheral vision.
Stiff-in-the-neck Scorpio
may not oblige,
cannot comply.

Squat under the
weight of
bloated self-absorbance
Scorpio's stinger misses.

Bleary-eyed
youth will stumble
through the
streets of old in
unromantic isolation.
The macrocosm wills it.

Earless Scorpio
retreats to a palace
of smoke and mirrors
with the dream that
the parochial is sufficient,
indigent.
Thin ice it seems,
but Scorpio slights it,
and when the weight of
waiting Karma yields to
Universal Law,
bitter brine will swallow it,
blunted, sterile stinger and all.

                                        –Debra Providence

Saturday Evenings

barefoot
she runs down the rocky dirt path
through the tall sharp blades of fever grass
through the shadows of the trees behind her
she runs through the oranges, the yellows,
the reds and mauves of the setting sun
she runs through the air filled with mangoes,
jarplums, guavas, and golden apples
she runs through the sounds of the crickets,
grasshoppers and other night creatures
and finally over the coconut tree trunk bridge

she heads to the checkered printed linoleum covered table
in a shed made of scraps of wood, bamboo,
coconut tree leaves, and galvanise
above the table resides a single bulb fixture
that attracts an array of flying creatures
seating consists of an old armchair, a wooden stool
an iron chair and an overturned bucket
this is where they gather every Saturday evening to
play dominoes

and soca music plays
while the cards are being shuffled
sunset rum perfumes the immediate air
while in a distance there's a faint smell of
breadfruit roasting for supper
conversations about the last cricket match
and the prime minister and about mrs. porter
granddaughter who's pregnant again
scatter about like the shuffling dominoes
but they too settle
as the match begins

                              —Jamillah Burgin

Versatile Woman

Easily identified by her multi-faceted prowess
Her latent strength many a man's weakness
Her smile is a frown is a scowl is a comfort
Strong and Powerful yet Fragile and Humble

Her words perpetuate wisdom and experience
Adeptly portrayed by her defiant obedience,
Obedience: to her person, staying true to herself
Lending her being to those who need help
Sharing her knowledge with all who want to hear
Putting up with nuisances only this temperament can bear
With a keen eye she roots out the troublemakers
And transforms little girls into professional bakers
And like a rainbow whose many hues make the show,
So too does this versatility makes this disposition glow.
A Mother A Nurse A Teacher A Politician
An Activist A Doctor A Lawyer
One Woman

–Janique-Ka John

I Am, Olivia Stephens
charcoal

Part of a self-portrait project entitled "I AM" exploring the African roots of
Caribbean identity, this drawing represents for me the inner resolve and strength
that emerges from the process of self-discovery. It communicates the resilience
that has shaped my character.

About the Contributors

Alisa Alvis. Alisa is a psychologist who works with at-risk youth. She writes to express her ideals concerning matters of social justice and is currently pursuing her Ph.D. in School Psychology at Syracuse University.

Narissa Ballantyne. Narissa graduated from SVG Community College in 2007 and is taking a Communication Studies degree at UWI, St. Augustine Campus.

Shanelle Bascombe. Shanelle graduated from SVG Community College in 2007 and is currently pursuing degree studies in sculpture and ceramics at Eduardo Abuela Escuela de Artes Plasticas, Cuba. She has been offered opportunities for further study in Cuba at the Institute Superior des Artes. On her return to St Vincent, Shanelle intends to establish a sculpture studio and teach.

Jamillah Burgin. Born in 1981, Jamillah has a BA in sociology from Manhattanville College and an MSc in Project Management from Lancaster University.

Shonette Bynoe. Shonette graduated from SVG Community College in 2007 and currently teaches visual arts at St. Martin's Secondary School, Kingstown.

Peggy Carr. Peggy is a journalist and poet who has been writing for many years. She won second prize in the BBC's Caribbean Poetry Competition and has published three volumes of poetry, the latest of which is *Honey and Lime.*

Amanda Frederick. Amanda graduated from SVG Community College in 2007 and teaches visual arts at St. Vincent Boys Grammar School, Kingstown.

Felicia Gabrielle George. Born in St. Vincent in 1991, Felicia attended the SVG Community College. She studied economics, sociology, communications studies, and literature.

Nelcia Robinson Hazell. Nelcia is a community educator. She has transferred her knowledge of Carib history and traditions into storytelling and is an authority on the indigenous peoples of the region. Her poetry spans 25 years.

Janeele Jackson. Janeele attended St. Joseph's Convent, Mesopotamia, and the St. Vincent Technical College. She has been writing since the age of 13.

Clare Ibberson-John. Clare became a citizen of St. Vincent in 2004. She has taught communication studies at the SVG Community College and is currently a tutor for the University of the West Indies and Kirklees College, Huddersfield.

Janique-Ka John. After graduating from SVG Community College in 2009, Janique-Ka freelanced as a journalist for *Searchlight* newspaper and is currently majoring in computer science at UWI Cave Hill campus.

Nerissa King. Nerissa graduated from SVG Community College in 2009 and currently teaches visual arts at St. Joseph's Convent, Kingstown.

Jecinta Hope Knights. Jecinta creates poems to accompany her dried flower collage work in greeting cards. She has exhibited combined works of art and poetry in Kingstown, London, New York, and Grenada. In Barbados she placed 2nd for best original creation at the Caribbean Draft Marketplace.

Jeneille Lewis. Born in 1983, Janeille attended Girls High School in St. Vincent; she graduated with a BA in History from the University of the Southern Caribbean in Trinidad. She is currently reading for a degree in law at the Kingston University, UK.

Joyce Peters McKenzie (deceased). Joyce was born in 1939 and worked as a high school teacher and administrator. Her work has been published in periodicals including "New Voices" and "Pathways". She authored a novel, *Man Born Ya.*

Natana McLean. Natana graduated from SVG Community College in 2007, obtained certification in permaculture design in 2008, and teaches visual arts at Emanuel High School, Kingstown.

Nora Peacock (deceased). Nora was editor of *The Vincentian* newspaper from 1973 to 1989. She wrote numerous incisive editorials and articles on the political and socio-economic situation of the country. She was an outspoken advocate on issues affecting women and an example of someone who used the power of the written word to effect change.

Debra Providence. Debra has published fiction and poetry in "POUI: The Cave Hill Literary Annual", the Cave Hill Campus Newspaper of the University of the West Indies, "Sable LitMag", and non-fiction in the "Journal of East Caribbean Studies". Her influences are Caribbean folk tradition, African American literary and popular culture, and science fiction and fantasy.

Vonnie Roudette. Vonnie relocated to St. Vincent from Trinidad in 1992. An artist/designer, she has free-lanced in textile, video art direction and theatre design in Japan, Europe, and the Caribbean. She resides in Penniston, and is a farmer/gardener, handcraft development consultant, and author of a collection of Caribbean nature essays entitled *Nature of Belonging*. She divides her time between teaching A-Level Art and Design at St.Vincent Community College, pioneering creative education projects for the youth, and writing.

Caroline "booops" Sardine. Having graduated in 1999 from the Edna Manley School of Visual and Performing Arts, Jamaica, "booops" subsequently received an MA from the Royal College of Art, London, in 2001. She exhibited her painting and assemblage at 'Young Talent V' at the Jamaica National Gallery in June 2010.

Olivia Stephens. Olivia graduated from SVG Community College in 2011. She is a regular host and panelist of "The Art Room", a weekly national youth radio program, and facilitates creativity workshops for children.

Author Index

www.ingramcontent.com/pod-product-compliance
Lightning Source LLC
Chambersburg PA
CBHW041408010726
47507CB00001B/37